SANTA FE AND TAOS, 1898-1942
An American Cultural Center

"The appeal of elements indigenous to the region played an indispensable role..."

Shepherd and Flock at St. Francis of Assisi Church in Taos. Photo courtesy Joe Munroe Visual Productions, Orinda, California.

SOUTHWESTERN STUDIES

MONOGRAPH NO. 67

Santa Fe and Taos
1898 - 1942
An American Cultural Center

by

Kay Aiken Reeve

COPYRIGHT 1982

TEXAS WESTERN PRESS
The University of Texas at El Paso

ISBN 0-87404-126-0

EDITORIAL BOARD

James M. Day, *Chairman*

William C. Cornell	Braja M. Das	Sharon Pontious
Fernando N. Garcia	Wayne E. Fuller	Z. A. Kruszewski
Fred W. Norwood		Joseph D. Olander

Hugh W, Treadwell, *Director*

ABOUT THE AUTHOR

Kay Aiken Reeve was born in Ft. Worth, Texas, and grew up in various Texas towns. Five years of her childhood, however, were spent in Farmington, New Mexico. That experience as well as annual visits to the family's summer cabin in Taos Canyon nurtured a deep and continuing interest in the Santa Fe-Taos region in particular and the American Southwest in general. After receiving her M.A. degree from Texas Tech University, she attended Texas A&M University where in 1977 she received a Ph.D. degree in American history with a specialization in the American West. She has served as a teaching assistant and instructor of history at Texas Tech and Texas A&M universities, and as a temporary assistant professor of history at Auburn University. She currently resides in Auburn, Alabama, with her husband T. Gilmour Reeve, an associate professor of physical education, and their son Bourke. The Reeve family continues to travel to the Southwest as often as possible to visit relatives and friends, refresh their love of the region, and in order for the author to continue her research in Western studies.

The views expressed in *Southwestern Studies* are those of the authors and not necessarily of Texas Western Press.

SANTA FE AND TAOS, 1898-1942: AN AMERICAN CULTURAL CENTER

by

Kay Aiken Reeve

WRITING in the 1830s of that part of the Mexican nation destined to become the state of New Mexico, Josiah Gregg declared, "There is no part of the civilized globe, perhaps, where the arts have been so much neglected."[1] In contrast to this bleak appraisal, by the 1920s the region of northern New Mexico surrounding Santa Fe and Taos was internationally recognized as a productive center of American literary and artistic activity. During the first several decades of the twentieth century these two small villages became the temporary or permanent home of dozens of painters, poets, novelists and sculptors who produced well accepted works in a variety of styles and mediums. Such a concentration of creative individuals, and the resulting formation of an "artist colony," was not a new phenomenon in the cultural history of the United States. The establishment of such a center in the remote heart of the American West, however, was a unique development. Why did this region — located far from publishers, galleries, patrons and markets — become a successful center of artistic productivity during those years?

There is certainly no lack of source material for those interested in the development of the Santa Fe-Taos cultural center. Within a few years of the establishment of the artist colony at Taos, articles about the artists of Santa Fe and Taos began to appear in popular and art-oriented magazines. While less frequently studied than the artists, the writers of the region had their chroniclers and critics as well.[2] In addition to works by "outsiders," by the very nature of their occupations the resident painters and authors produced an enormous collection of memoirs, essays, novels, and paintings interpreting their chosen place of residence and its hold upon them. Despite this vast volume of source material, or perhaps because of it, a completely satisfactory explanation as to why the center flourished so heartily between 1900 and 1940 has been elusive. Emphasis on one particular artist or on one specific characteristic of the region has often led to an over-simplification of the appeal of the area. In reality a complex variety of environmental and cultural factors, some native to northern New Mexico and others arriving with the incoming artists and authors, intertwined and interacted to support both the establishment and the continuing productivity of the center. The unique combination of elements which contributed to the success of the Santa Fe-Taos cultural center deserves a more complete analysis than it has yet received, for a better understanding of the reasons for the flourishing of the center would serve to illuminate not only the particular appeal of Santa Fe and Taos, but also the aesthetic appeal of the entire American West. Similarly, a clearer understanding of the appeal of the region to the artists would help to more fully define the character of the cultural and intellectual climate of the United States during much of the first four decades of this century.

THE ESTABLISHMENT OF THE CENTER

The development of the Santa Fe-Taos region as a center of literary and artistic activity began shortly before the start of the twentieth century with the creation of an artist colony in Taos.[3] In 1898 Bert G. Phillips and Ernest L. Blumenschein, two academically trained New York artists, headed west in order to escape what they considered to be the overwhelming influence of European art and art education upon American painters of the period. They were so thrilled by the beauty and indigenous character of the land and peoples they discovered in Taos that they cancelled their plans to continue on to old Mexico and instead painted in the village through the fall. Indeed, Bert Phillips settled in Taos that year, becoming its first permanent resident artist. During the next forty years the artist colony in the town grew steadily. Joseph Henry Sharp, nationally recognized for his paintings of Plains Indians and a previous visitor to the town, settled permanently in Taos in 1912. W. Herman Dunton, Oscar Berninghaus, and E. Irving Couse, three successful illustrators-turned-painters with an interest in painting Indians and the American West, and the Chicago artists Walter Ufer and Victor Higgins all settled in Taos between 1912 and 1927. Traditionalists, both academically and stylistically, were in the vanguard of artists to arrive, and traditionalism continued to represent the orientation of the majority of the artists in the colony.[4] Yet while traditionally "Western" paintings were most often produced in the colony, growth and development brought about changes of style for some painters, and the arrival of artists with diverse backgrounds and styles further altered the colony. Leon Gaspard and Nicolai Fechin, both Russian born and trained, came via New York to add the elements of impressionism and expressionistic portraiture to the Taos colony. In the late 1920s and the 1930s the arrival of Andrew Dasburg, Thomas Benrimo, and Emil Bisttram brought distinctly modernistic styles to the village. Thus through the years the artistic community in Taos both grew and diversified.

During these same years another colony of artists took root seventy miles to the south in Santa Fe. As in Taos, the earliest artists to settle in the village were academically trained realists. Sheldon Parsons, Carlos Vierra, and Gerald Cassidy were all living and working in Santa Fe by 1914. In some ways never as cohesive a "colony" as the Taos artists, the gathering of artists in Santa Fe nevertheless increased in size over the years, and the group diversified even more rapidly than did its northern counterpart. Between 1913 and 1920 Paul Burlin, a participant in the momentous Armory Show of February 1913, made Santa Fe his home. Other modernists in the town included Raymond Jonson, B.J.O. Nordfeldt, Walter Mruk, and Joseph Bakos. William Penhallow Henderson and Fremont Ellis added the elements of expressionism and impressionism, while John Sloan's decision to make Santa Fe his permanent summer residence added even more prestige to the colony. Although the trip between the two towns was difficult, especially in the early years, the two groups of artists were friendly and interacted frequently.

The artists' opportunities for interaction with creative contemporaries were increased by the development during these same years of active literary colonies in the two towns. Between 1916 and 1940 numerous writers of national reputation were frequent visitors to the region, and several became permanent residents. Alice Corbin Henderson, co-founder with Harriet Monroe of *Poetry: A Magazine of Verse* and an active Chicago poet and editor, moved to Santa Fe in 1916. The well known California author Mary Austin resettled there in 1924. Mabel Dodge, once cited as having established the "only successful salon" ever attempted in America,[5] arrived in Taos in late 1916 as the wife of painter Maurice Sterne. After divorcing Sterne, she stayed to become the wife of Tony Luhan, a Pueblo Indian, and to play a vital role in attracting to New Mexico many of the most creative people of her era. A fairly prolific writer herself, she added even more to the literary reputation of the region when she brought to Taos its most famous temporary resident, D.H. Lawrence. Lawrence lived in New Mexico for almost three years between 1922 and 1926, and was hoping to return permanently when he died in Italy.

Other well known poets and novelists visited the area, including John Gould Fletcher, Willa Cather, and Carl Sandburg. Frank Waters, "Spud" Johnson, Witter Bynner, and Haniel Long settled permanently in Santa Fe or Taos.[6] Thus by the 1920s the Santa Fe-Taos region of New Mexico was recognized nationally as a blossoming center of artistic and literary activity.

REASONS FOR THE CENTER'S DEVELOPMENT

The original impetus for visiting or settling in Taos or Santa Fe varied greatly among the incoming artists. Some came seeking "fresh material;" others came as semi-invalids seeking a healthful climate; still others came at the invitation of earlier arrivals. Despite the diversity of the original purpose in visiting the region and the variety of artistic styles and medium which developed in the center, the works produced and the statements of the artists themselves attest to the fact that several elements basic to the northern New Mexican environment held universal appeal for the newcomers. The most pervasively influential of these were the magnificent physical environment, the Pueblo Indian culture, and the Spanish-American culture.[7] Similarly pervasive was the fact that the initial appeal of all these elements was visual in nature.

The northern New Mexican environment displayed a landscape of remarkable color and diversity to the incoming artists. The high, dry atmosphere of Santa Fe and Taos intensified light and clarified form. Desert, mountain, and mesa changed coloration and mood with the hour of the day or the season of the year. For painters in particular the outstanding clarity and brightness of light in the Santa Fe-Taos area served to stimulate and challenge creative efforts. Marsden Hartley, who painted in the Taos area in 1918 and 1919, wrote perceptively of the intensity of light he experienced there. New Mexico was not, he said, "a country of light on things" but was rather "a country of things in light."[8] John Marin, another fine artist who spent two summers in Taos, also noted the unique quality of light in the region. He wrote, "If you think you know what light is then go to New Mexico and you'll find a light many times more intense than anything you get in New York, or Maine, or the White Mountains."[9] For some artists, especially during their initial experience with it, the bright light of New Mexico was almost overpowering. Once that impact had been successfully weathered, however, many artists found the brightness and clarity of atmosphere and the vividness of colors to be among the most appealing and stimulating features of the region's environment.

Authors who came to northern New Mexico in the early years of the twentieth century were also struck by the exceptional beauty of the area. When asked in 1932 to explain why she had chosen to live in Santa Fe, Mary Austin asserted that three things tied her firmly to the town. The first of these was the immense and dramatic beauty of the mountainous country surrounding the village.[10] Mabel Dodge Luhan, writing of her first trip from Santa Fe through the Rio Grande Valley to Taos, recalled the profound impact which the region's beauty had upon her, and how it brought to mind the singularly fitting quotation, " 'Tis the beauty not the strangeness turns the traveler's heart to stone."[11] More simply, D. H. Lawrence expressed what many artists felt when he declared, "There are all kinds of beauty in this world . . . But for a greatness of beauty I have never experienced anything like New Mexico."[12]

For most of the newly arrived artists and authors the visual appeal of the environment was matched by that of the native peoples of New Mexico. Particularly fascinating were the Pueblo Indians. By the early years of the twentieth century the Pueblos of New Mexico were living in nineteen communal villages called pueblos. Sixteen were located in the Rio Grande Valley, with three others farther west. There were an additional eight pueblo villages of the Hopi in Arizona.[13] An attractive people, the Pueblos were of medium height with coppery complexions, broad foreheads, and massive cheekbones. Their straight black hair was worn by the men in long braids, and by the women gathered at the neck with heavy bangs across the forehead. Color was the keynote of their traditional style of clothing. The men dressed in brightly colored shirts, often of calico, and trousers of heavy cloth or hide with a vertical string of fringe below the knee. Brightly colored blankets were always worn or carried. Women wore short *mantas* over muslin underdresses. Woven belts, moccasins with high deerskin leggings, and colored shawls completed the outfit. Perhaps even more colorful were the various ceremonial dance costumes, which included wings of eagle feathers and headdresses of antlers. The visual appeal of such a people was immediate, intense, and enduring. In 1898, Ernest Blumenschein spoke of the appeal of the "picturesque, colorful, [Pueblos], dressed in blankets artistically draped."[14] Barbara Latham, who arrived in Taos twenty-seven years after Blumenschein, recalled that one of her first impressions was of the "color and design" — elements she considered to be the basics of her painting — she saw displayed in the Indians' dress and culture.[15] An attractive and colorful people, the Pueblo Indians and their traditional culture provided stimulating subject matter for the artists and writers of the region.

The Spanish-American people, like the Pueblo, also offered elements which immediately appealed to the incoming artists as colorful subject matter. In Hispanic homes artists saw brightly colored handwoven blankets and rugs spread beneath primitively carved and painted images of the dying Christ. In Santa Fe and Taos, as in the more remote mountain villages, the artists were surrounded by a pleasantly "foreign atmosphere created by the presence of the Spanish-Americans" in the area.[16] Foreign too (for artists wearied of urban

America) were delightful scenes of firewood laden donkeys being driven down dusty trails into town, for even in the early twentieth century "all the wood for Santa Fe still came down from the mountains on burroback."[17] The weathered face of the sheepherder, so long exposed to the semi-arid environment; black-shawled women or shy, dark-eyed children — "always polite and respectful, yet so full of fun;"[18] the earthen homes of the Hispanos; all these reflections of the Spanish-American culture immediately offered colorful and stimulating subjects. The Hispanos, like the Pueblo Indians and the striking physical environment, presented vivid scenes for the newly arrived painters or authors to capture.

Despite the stimulation of the beauty and color of the region and its native inhabitants, to assert that the visual appeal of the natural environment and of the Spanish-American and Pueblo Indian peoples alone caused the establishment and continued development of the center is to oversimplify both the qualities of the New Mexican environment and peoples, and the motivations of the incoming artists. Certainly for some artists, especially those traditionalists who came to the region intending to document an Indian culture or Western environment which they feared was doomed, the faithful rendering of an appealing subject remained a sufficient goal. Many other artistic emigrants, however, sought to develop a fuller understanding of their new home and neighbors, and as they did so discovered elements which they admired not merely for their beauty, but more deeply for their intrinsic value. To the artists who came to the region seeking something more than "fresh material," many qualities of the New Mexican land and native peoples offered direct contrasts to qualities in the dominant American culture which they found disturbing.[19] Thus external and internal factors combined to deepen the appeal which the environment, the Pueblo Indians, and the Spanish-Americans held for the newly arrived Anglo authors and painters.

ENVIRONMENT OF NORTHERN NEW MEXICO

The Elemental Character of the Land

For those artists for whom the appeal of the environment extended far beyond its external beauty, several characteristics of the region were particularly influential. Among these characteristics the one which exerted the most profound effect was the elemental character of the land. In northern New Mexico the landscape seemed reduced to its simplest and most basic forms. Concurrently, the relationship of these forms seemed structured by an intrinsic and all powerful order. Positive artistic reaction to this quality of the environment was evident in the works of members of both the art and literary colonies of Taos and Santa Fe, but those painters associated with various modernistic movements of the period seemed most deeply affected. Andrew Dasburg, Emil Bisttram and Raymond Jonson all drew particular inspiration from the inherent order and form displayed in the region's landscape. Dasburg, as a proponent of the work of Cézanne and Matisse, was already recognized as a "modernist" when he arrived in Taos in 1918. Jonson and Bisttram were destined to follow their early interest in modern art into a dedication to abstract art during their long years in New Mexico. Each of these artists acknowledged the particularly important role that the nature of the New Mexican landscape played in the development of their styles.

Andrew Dasburg first came to Taos at the invitation of his friends, painter Maurice Sterne and Mabel Dodge, then Mrs. Sterne. Although he came without intending to paint or draw, he was immediately captivated by the dramatic environment of the area. In New Mexico, Dasburg found geometric forms prominently displayed in adobe buildings, irrigated fields, and pine covered mountains. All of these forms were uniquely illumined by the brilliant light of the region. For more than half a century Dasburg explored the forms and shapes of the New Mexican environment in a style that combined elements of cubism and a Cézannesque color treatment, coupled with a highly personal interpretation of line, color, order and space. While Dasburg experimented with abstraction early in his career he later returned to a style of expression he considered more ordered and personally fulfilling.[20] He found the landscape of the region the perfect stimulus for the creation of compositions he called "compromises between reality and the abstract."[21]

In contrast, Emil Bisttram and Raymond Jonson believed the environment helped nurture their stylistic change to total abstraction. For Bisttram, inspiration came as much from what he felt in the region — "the rhythms and vibrations produced by the land" — as he defined it, as from what he saw.[22] In his paintings he sought to create "universal and cosmic forms representative of mental, emotional, and spiritual experience."[23] Similarly, Raymond Jonson discovered in New Mexico an environment which supported his earlier dedication to "Design and Order," as he personally conceived them, and helped further his steady stylistic move from semirepresentational to total abstraction. For ten years following his move to Santa Fe from Chicago Jonson produced hundreds of sketches of the hills, mesas, and the fascinating effects of erosion upon the land. These "finger exercises," the artist explained, served to acquaint him spiritually with the forms, shapes, and rhythms of New Mexico. This experimentation culminated in the production of a series of sixteen abstract paintings he described as "syntheses." Rather than representing a particular setting, each was "a new type of landscape that objectively and visually had nothing to do with the three dimensional landscape, [but represented] a synthetic abstraction of old feelings and excitements based on the objective landscape."²⁴ In Jonson's consistent attempt to move beyond the immediate to the universal the physical setting in which he worked was especially influential. The artist himself insisted that his mature style, with its prime emphasis on design, order, and color, could not have developed in any environment other than that of northern New Mexico.

While the fundamental forms and order displayed in the New Mexican environment appealed most strongly to modernistic painters, the effect was certainly not limited to them. Mabel Dodge Luhan wrote in praise of life in Taos for its revelation of the inherent sense of order and orderly progression which nature dictates. *Winter in Taos* described the characteristics of each season and catalogued the changing moods and responsibilities the seasons brought to a Taos resident.²⁵ More importantly, Mrs. Luhan believed the structured relations and measured passage of time displayed in the New Mexican environment revealed the innate order of the universe and the proper relationship of man to man and man to nature. This "regulated relationship of one to all and all to one" she called "Significant Form". It was "Significant Form," she asserted, that artists were "perpetually trying to find and project upon their canvases," and it was "Significant Form" with which the artist was surrounded in northern New Mexico.²⁶

The Scope and Age of the Land

Two other basic qualities of the physical environment deeply affected many of the artists and writers of the center. The vastness of scope and the seeming timelessness of the forces of nature became fundamental themes in many of the works produced in Santa Fe and Taos. Many perceptive individuals felt that the scope and age of the mountain and desert landscape tended to place man in his proper perspective with nature. Paul Burlin asserted that in New Mexico "man's stature was always diminutive," while John Marin wrote from Taos to a New York friend that New Mexico was a land of "Big Sun heat. Big storm. Big everything. — A leaving out that thing called man."[27]

While the effect of the vast scope of the landscape is evident in many of Burlin and Marin's New Mexico paintings, the intensity of impact which that quality of the environment can have is revealed most clearly in the works of Georgia O'Keeffe. A summer resident of the region beginning in 1929, she settled permanently in New Mexico in 1946 after the death of her husband, the pioneering New York photographer and art critic Alfred Stieglitz. All of her unique landscapes emphasize the vast scope of their subject, but the elements of scope and timelessness are most distinctly seen in her compositions of bleached cowskulls and bones surrealistically imposed above a stark desert landscape. The frequent inclusion of flowers in these paintings reveals that their theme is not the destructive character of nature, but rather the sense of the eternal which radiates from the endless continuance of life even in the heart of the desert.[28]

The impact of the scope and age of the environment was also a recurring theme in the works of regional authors. The effect that the Southwestern vastness could have upon the spirit of a receptive individual was explored by Alice Corbin in the poem entitled "Three Men Entered the Desert Alone." Two of the men traveling through the desert seemed unaffected, ". . . while the third felt his soul grow vast/as the circle of sand and alkalie./His soul extended and touched the sky. . ."[29] In "El Rito de Santa Fe" the same poet reflected upon the overpowering sense of timelessness which the land exuded. Writing at first of the ancient and unknown people who had inhabited the land before the present occupants, the last stanza puts even that period of time in proper perspective with regard to the age of the land itself. The poet suggests,

> Let us build a monument to Time
> That knows all, sees all, and contains all,
> To whom these bones in the valley are even as we are:
> Even Time's monument would crumble
> Before the face of Time. . . .[30]

The Artists' Bond with the Land

Vast scope, a sense of the eternal, elemental structure, and innate order were all qualities of the New Mexican environment which inspired the artists and authors who arrived in the area during the first decades of the twentieth century. Beyond even these elements, some of the creative individuals who settled there felt that there existed in the area an indefinable quality, a spiritual "something else," that tied them most firmly to the Santa Fe-Taos region. Mabel Luhan conceived the power in mystical terms, and wrote of its anonymous appeal in an article entitled "Paso Por Aqui," and in her last book, *Taos and Its Artists.* She asserted that a "mysterious gravitation" impelled sensitive individuals to come to Taos and to react to the environment. That same force, the "Genius Loci" of the valley, as she called it, reigned as a benign and tolerant force in Taos Valley, and sought to stimulate the creative impulse. Just as this force attracted and nourished the creative, it drove away those whose "essential nature" was destructive.[31] Similarly, Emil Bisttram believed that a spiritual force nurtured and encouraged creativity in Taos Valley. Bisttram, who formulated a unique personal religion incorporating elements of Oriental philosophy and mysticism, believed that he had been fated to discover Taos, and to make the village his home. Taos, he believed, was destined to become the creative center of the United States because Taos Mountain was the home of one of the five benevolent spirits which seek to guide mankind. The presence of this spirit radiated a magnetic, creative energy which those who were in tune could feel vibrating within the very earth in the Santa Fe-Taos region.[32] Yet whether the creative emigrant conceived the force in mystical or concrete terms, most artists received a powerful inspiration from the northern New Mexican environment.

Attractive in its own right, for many artists the importance of the possibility of such an emotional or spiritual bond with the land was intensified by the seeming inability of the dominant American society of the period to provide such a link. By the early years of the twentieth century industrialization and urbanization in the United States seemed to have created a "rootless" society. Traditional values and institutions that had been mainstays of agrarian America had been abandoned. Ties to family and community were disappearing. Many individuals were, as Mabel Luhan described them, "people who float around the world . . . looking for climates or distractions, or something." She herself had been such a person, a spirit "hovering over the earth," until she discovered in Taos a place where she could put down roots.[33] Indeed, its elemental nature and long history gave the New Mexican earth a quality of depth which seemed to invite the newcomer to take root. In northern New Mexico many individuals found a home where, like Mrs. Luhan, they felt a bond with the earth, and where they drew creative nourishment from the land. In their paintings, poems, novels, and essays these artists attempted to communicate to the rest of society the strength and contentment they had gained from attachment to the American land.

THE PUEBLO INDIAN CULTURE

In the same way that artists were influenced by both the visual appeal of the physical environment and by a deeper bond with the New Mexican land, the native peoples of the area attracted the artist on two levels. Obviously the external color of the Pueblo Indians — his dress, dances, art, architecture — provided stimulating visual experiences for all the artists of Taos and Santa Fe. For many artists, however, the appeal of the Indian was soon more firmly grounded in a deeper admiration for various qualities inherent in Pueblo culture. Although the Pueblos were divided physically and linguistically into several groups and never considered themselves a unified tribe or nation, numerous social and ceremonial traditions and religious beliefs were shared by all Pueblo peoples. Also shared was the significant accomplishment of having preserved well into the twentieth century many traditional customs, beliefs, and ceremonies in their ancient form. As the incoming artists gained a fuller understanding of Pueblo tradition, many discovered that they admired the culture as much for its intrinsic worth as for its external beauty.

The Pueblo Religion

Among the most universally appealing elements of the Pueblo culture was its religion, a faith which represented the most enduring and pervasive of all components of the Indian culture.[34] By the middle of the eighteenth century the majority of Pueblo Indians professed the Catholic faith; each pueblo had its own church, particular guardian saint, and special feast days. Concurrently, however, most Pueblos continued to adhere to their ancient Indian beliefs. Catholicism had been superimposed upon Pueblo religion without basically altering the function, the form, or the importance of the traditional religion. For the Pueblo Indian, religion transcended all other aspects of life. Art, drama, social organization, architecture, and even the everyday industries of life were affected. The Indian's whole life was ordered and shaped by his religion, the central tenet of which was its unique concept of man's unity with the universe. The Pueblo believed in a oneness of life as manifested in all things. Plants, animals, mountains, clouds, skies, and waters all shared equally with man the life force or great life principle. The Indian was part of nature, one element among many, rather than the master of all creation. This concept required that the Pueblo remain in the proper relationship with all of his surrounding environment, and a complex and extensive Pueblo legendry, ceremonial life, and communal social structure evolved from his efforts to do so.

The Pueblos' belief in the elemental unity of spirit in man, animal, and nature held particular appeal for many of the Anglo newcomers, and the harmony between the Indian and his environment was a frequent theme for Taos and Santa Fe painters and writers. B. J. O. Nordfeldt, Howard Cook, William P. Henderson, and Lady Dorothy Brett all painted studies of Pueblo Indians designed to communicate the sense of unity with nature manifested in the Pueblos' customs and way of life. Even the modernist painter Raymond Jonson was particularly impressed by this feature of Pueblo culture.[35] In the 1930s, before his style became entirely abstract, Jonson produced two series of semi-abstract paintings, entitled "Pueblo Series" and "Cliff Dwellings," composed of highly stylized paintings of Pueblo villages. Each revealed the remarkable harmony between the dwellings and the surrounding environment. For example, in his painting "Cliff Dwelling, No. 3,"[36] the ruin of an ancient pueblo is actually placed inside the cliff which dominates the center of the picture, thus graphically showing how the manmade structure functioned as an integral part of nature.

The Indian's unity with nature was also an important theme in the literature produced in the region. D. H. Lawrence wrote of that unique quality in his essay "New Mexico." In New Mexico, Lawrence asserted, he had discovered many things of great value. Among these was the distinctive religion of the Pueblo Indians. He used the term a "vast old religion," and wrote of it as "starkly and nakedly religious." In Pueblo religion nature shared with man the spirit which white men would identify as divinity, but his belief was not, Lawrence asserted,

> the pantheism we are accustomed to, which expresses itself as 'God is everywhere, God is in everything.' In the oldest religion, everything was alive, not supernaturally but naturally alive. There were only deeper and deeper streams of life. . . .[37]

The Indian's life was merely one part of this cosmic life, and the right relationship was one of harmony and unity. As his religion was inseparable from his life, the Pueblo revealed this relationship even in his secular activities. Lawrence was struck by this and recalled that "When Trinidad, the Indian boy, and I planted corn at the ranch my soul paused to see his hands softly moving the earth over the maize in pure ritual."[38]

A similar theme often appeared in the works of Mabel Dodge Luhan. From the time of her earliest experiences with the Pueblo Indians Mrs. Luhan sensed qualities within their lives which seemed to be painfully lacking in her own. Indeed, she felt that a majority of members of her race lived lives lacking the wisdom of the Indian. The Indian's life seemed "Real, real and deep as fate, full of wisdom and experience."[39] The Indian understood his role in the world, his relationship to the other elements of the universe. The Pueblos, she asserted rather mystically,

> Know they are themselves the earth and the rain and the sun. . . . We (the white race) watch things happen in nature as though they were outside of us and separate from us, but the Indians know they are what they contemplate.[40]

The Ceremonial Dances

Among the Pueblo activities which outwardly reflected their religious beliefs the ones most frequently painted by Anglo artists were the ceremonial dances. The dances were favorite sources of inspiration not only because they were so colorful, but also because they so clearly expressed the Indian's concept of universal unity and interdependence of man and nature. Performed throughout the changing seasons and associated with almost every aspect of Pueblo life, dances were observed at the proper time and in the proper costume as the Pueblos' contribution to the maintenance of the harmony of nature.

Of the many artists who painted the dances, William P. Henderson of Santa Fe was particularly successful in capturing the rhythm, movement, and mood of the dancers. Less concerned with literal documentation as with interpretation, his paintings presented an expressive reality characterized by particularly strong, vivid colors that reflected the strength and vitality of the dances. An interesting example of his interpretive approach to the dances is presented in his "Walpi Snake Dance".[41] All the elements which in truth are part of the ceremony — dancers with white painted faces carrying snakes, the feathers used to stroke the serpent, and the sacred blue corn meal sprinkled on the snakes — appear in the picture, yet these elements have been arranged by the artist so as to express rhythm, mood, and meaning. The setting for the dancers and their audience, the typical collection of women and older men, is the desert outside the pueblo rather than the pueblo plaza. The desert setting emphasizes the Hopi's particularly intense need for the gifts of the gods, especially the gift of rain. Level yellow and orange desert stretches far away to a horizon of flat-topped pink and blue mesas. The only sign of plant life appears in the form of a branch covered with rounded green leaves placed in the left foreground just above the row of dancers. Some of these leaves circle the waist and head of the Indian holding the blue corn and feather, symbolizing the Hopi's belief in the inseparability of the ceremonies and fertility. Henderson's suggestive use of color even extends to the variation in the coloring of his human subjects. The Hopi women, all of whom are wearing the distinctive hair style of young women of that people, are painted in a light golden shade. The older men who are watching the dance, having participated when they were younger, are painted in a darker shade. But the skin of the dancers themselves is a deep redbrown, reflecting the strength, power, and vitality which the Indian draws from the enactment of the ancient ritual and his communion with the forces of nature.

While at times it may have been difficult for the artist to separate inspiration gained from the beauty of the dances and that of their role as expressions of Pueblo belief, their importance as both art and religion was definitely appreciated. In 1923, when action by the Federal government threatened to destroy the dances, Alice Corbin Henderson wrote a perceptive article for *Theater Arts Magazine* in which she discussed the dances as art, drama, and religious ritual unified. The dances, she asserted, were symbolic interpretations of the Indian's conception of "man's relation to the earth, and to the fructifying principles of sun, wind, and water." They represented also "a perfect art form [which was] the result of centuries of tradition, an expression of an esthetic philosophy of life which flows into outward symbols and gestures."[42] As drama the dances were unique and instructive, in that they were performed without regard for or need of an audience, for they were performed for the participants, not the onlookers. In this feature, they were similar to the goat dances and nature festivals which were the foundation of Greek drama. Thus, Mrs. Henderson noted,

> As a background for the study of sources of drama they are worth a whole library of text-books; and in themselves they constitute a living organism, a beautiful and vital art, persisting in the face of discouragement and under constant threat of suppression.[43]

They persisted despite government policy, she asserted, for they were not only artistic expressions, but also religious ones.

The Communal Spirit of the Indian

The Indian's concept of the interrelatedness of all elements of creation also affected his relations with his fellow man. His beliefs created a sense of community with men as well as nature. This communal spirit was clearly manifested in his relationship with the immediate community, his particular pueblo. Although all the Pueblos had occasionally united for common action, as during the Pueblo Revolt of 1680, traditionally the individual Pueblo Indian's loyalty was to his own pueblo and to its members. Of particular importance to him was his family, which for all Pueblos was an extended family unit, including grandparents and married children. In addition to his devotion to his family, the Pueblo felt a communal tie to the other members of the pueblo, and an abiding bond with his pueblo as an entity. Although there was no common ownership of crops or other personal property, land was owned by the community and its use was granted to individuals or families. Each village member worked on communal projects, especially irrigation systems, and performed his role in communal ceremonies. Individualism existed, but the Pueblo's final responsibility was to the group, and the Indian conceived of himself as at once and inseparably an individual and a community member. Indeed, the Pueblo's sense of unity with nature and the members of his community was even reflected in the architecture of his village. Formed from the clay soil of the region, adobe dwellings echoed the natural forms which surrounded them. Great communal houses, some rising several stories high, contained the rooms of dozens of families. Individual lives were lived as an integral part of the whole. The Pueblo's bond with his people and with nature, a natural outgrowth of his religion, was thus reinforced even by the physical structure in which he lived.[44]

Many of the artists and authors who settled in Santa Fe and Taos were deeply impressed by the Pueblo's sense of community, and the value of the Indian's communal spirit became an important theme in the works of several of the region's writers and painters. Writing of the Pueblo's sense of unity with his people, Mary Austin asserted that the Pueblos represented "a society in which there is no partition between cultural and economic interests." Indeed, she viewed the Pueblo community as "the only organized group on earth in which group-mindedness runs higher than the individual reach."[45] It was this feeling of oneness with nature and his people which gave the individual Pueblo a unique wholeness of identity. Mrs. Austin expressed this view again in a private letter to Alice Corbin Henderson. In discussing Sherwood Anderson's *Mid-American Chants*,[46] Mrs. Austin praised the poems for their strengths, but contended that their major weakness was the poet's failure to recognize the depth of the Indian's communal bonds, so that "though the Indian sang only to his god, he sang out of a tribal experience more unified than anything we [Anglo society] know."[47]

Mabel Luhan also stressed the communal aspect of Pueblo character in her writings. Mrs. Luhan asserted that American society should learn from the Pueblos that the constant drive toward individualism, toward "more singleness, separateness, and individuality," was destroying "patterns of social and family life" throughout America. What was needed in American society was a sense of community and harmony with one's fellow man. Almost as a plea to the dominant Anglo-Saxon culture, she declared:

> Oh fellow mortal out there in the world! Until you learn how to join together once more, to fuse your sorrowful and lonely hearts in some new communion, you can never make true music. The sound you will produce will continue to be the agonized expression . . . of separate and unshared life.[48]

Pueblo Indian Art

While the Indian's sense of community with nature and his people held a particularly powerful appeal for the incoming artists, they were also attracted by other features of Pueblo culture. As artists it was natural for the newcomers to admire a culture in which art, religious expression, and daily life were not relegated to separate spheres. The ceremonial dances were a form of artistic expression as well as a religious one. Pueblo pottery and painting, while often used for ceremonial purposes, were inseparably art forms as well, and were admired as such by the Anglo artists. Although both pottery making and painting as traditional art forms had suffered an extreme decline during the nineteenth century, both arts were undergoing successful revivals by the early years of the twentieth century.[49] Many of the artists began collecting Pueblo pottery. Some used the pots as subjects in their paintings, but others collected them purely as works of art. The poet Witter Bynner made an extensive collection which was displayed in his home alongside his Chinese art and artifacts. Other newcomers, including Mary Austin, Mabel Luhan, Andrew Dasburg, and William and Alice Henderson, collected Pueblo paintings as well as pottery. These artists recognized the value of Pueblo paintings as art, not as anthropological objects. As an outgrowth of this concept of Pueblo painting John Sloan, supported by other Santa Fe residents, arranged in 1921 the first American showing of Indian paintings as works of art rather than as museum pieces.[50] This successful New York showing helped bring about the formation of a national organization, The Exposition of Indian Tribal Arts. The avowed purpose of the association was:

> To present Indian art *as art*; to win for it the appreciation that it deserves, and to gain the general recognition and appraisal for the art of our native

first Americans, which has been so generously accorded to the primitive and folk art of every other race and country.[51]

Even while they were engaged in activities designed to support and encourage Pueblo painting and pottery, the artists of Santa Fe and Taos were aware that they were not merely giving, but were very definitely receiving from the Pueblo's art. While the Anglo artists neither wished to copy the Indian style of painting nor to have the Indians copy the Anglo [European] style, individual elements of Pueblo art significantly influenced particular artists. As a modernistic painter Paul Burlin found the Indian use of design especially stimulating. His study of the abstract element in Indian art resulted in attempts to incorporate into his own work the direct yet nonobjective artistic expression he felt was inherent in Indian art forms.[52] Similarly, Raymond Jonson was particularly impressed by the symbolic designs used on Pueblo pottery. Jonson seldom used Indian designs as such in his work, but rather found them to be a stimulus to analyze his own use of design. He attempted, he later declared, to establish "Pure design" in his paintings at the same level of intensity that he saw it displayed in Pueblo art.[53]

While individual elements of Pueblo art affected particular artists especially strongly, the most pervasive influence of Pueblo art upon the painters and writers of the Santa Fe-Taos center stemmed from its indigenous character. In Pueblo painting, pottery, music, and dance Anglo artists saw artistic expressions of an indigenous people whose inspiration came from an ancient religious faith and intimate interaction with their native environment. As such, John Sloan and other artists maintained, Indian art represented a truly American aesthetic tradition.[54] Importantly, such a tradition represented something for which many artists of the period were personally searching, and something which they felt was lacking in American art in general. During the early years of the twentieth century many American artists began to feel a strong reaction against the pervasive influence which European art had on almost all aspects of art in the United States. There was a growing desire among artists, authors as well as painters, to create what they considered to be truly American art. In the art world for example, Alfred Stieglitz encouraged the development of modern art in the United States both for its own merits and because it was breaking with Europeanized academic style. He opened a series of galleries in New York City and arranged exhibitions for several modernistic American artists. His deep concern for the development of an aesthetic approach freed from dependence on Europe was displayed in his choice of a name for his last and most daring art gallery, "An American Place."[55]

Similarly, many writers of the period were beginning to break from the nineteenth century literary tradition which owed so much to European styles. Although not all would become "Literary Radicals," as Van Wyck Brooks described Randolph Bourne, many would have agreed with Bourne's assessment that "Our cultural humility is the chief obstacle. . . With our eyes fixed on Europe we continue to strangle whatever native genius springs up."[56] Thus, there was an active response to the call for writers to seek out a "usable past" on which to build a distinctly American literary tradition freed from imitation of European models. In many ways this drive lent support to the upsurge of "Regionalism" in literature during the period.[57] However, in literature as in painting, the most basic goal remained the development of a truly American artistic aesthetic. The strength of this element within the general artistic climate of the priod had an important impact on the development of the cultural center in Santa Fe and Taos, for it served to greatly intensify the appeal of the Pueblo Indians, their culture, and their homeland because they were so distinctly indigenous.

THE SPANISH-AMERICAN CULTURE

The incoming artists' interest in contact with indigenous cultures helped to strengthen their favorable reaction to the other native people of northern New Mexico, the Spanish-Americans. The ancestors of the Spanish-Americans, or Hispanos as they were often called, had entered the area more than 350 years earlier, and had settled near Santa Fe a decade before the founding of Jamestown. Despite the influence of the influx of Missouri traders down the Santa Fe Trail after 1821, the annexation of the territory by the United States in 1848, and the increasing number of Anglo residents in the region, the Hispanos retained well into the twentieth century many elements of their traditional culture. While the Hispanic culture of northern New Mexico was similar to the Spanish culture of Mexico and Latin America, it was in many ways a unique culture.[58] Long centuries of the relative isolation of the region resulted in the Hispano's retention of some cultural elements dating back to the seventeenth century. Similarly, this isolation allowed distinctive shaping of the culture by the unique New Mexican environment and by close contact with the Pueblo Indians. Among the most deeply embedded elements of the Spanish-American culture as it developed in New Mexico were the Hispano's intensely felt ties to his land and his family, his sense of community with his neighbors, and his simple yet devout Catholicism. These characteristics were still vital elements in the lives of the Hispanic people of the region during the early years of the twentieth century. As the artists and writers who settled in Santa Fe and Taos came into daily contact with these native New Mexicans they discovered much that they admired in the enduring Spanish-American culture.

Hispanic Adobe Architecture

As was true their reaction to the Indian culture, among the first elements of the Hispano culture to attract the newcomers' favorable attention were Spanish-American arts and crafts. While not strictly an art form, the handicraft of the Hispanos which was most prevalently displayed in the region was adobe architecture. Originally a Pueblo Indian building material, early Spanish settlers rapidly adopted the use of adobe. Working with the materials indigenous to the land, the Spanish made use of earth, brush, and abundant heat of the sun, and the less abundant pine and aspen trees of the mountains to construct their dwellings.[59] While styles changed somewhat through the years, adobe remained the basic element in Hispanic construction.

The appeal of adobe architecture to the artist lay in both its physical form and its essential nature. Handbuilt without the aid of level or plumb, adobe buildings had soft lines and curved corners. The covering plaster bore the mark of the hands that smoothed it, a characteristic which fascinated Easterners accustomed to more impersonal structures of stone or wooden planking. An adobe home seemed to be, as the Santa Fe artist Fremont Ellis commented, more "a sculpture which grows from the earth" than a building artificially placed upon it.[60] It was the indigenous character of the material which appealed most to those who viewed the houses not as "mud-huts," as many of the early travelers on the Santa Fe Trail had called them, but as natural, fitting, outgrowths of the landscape.

The very simplicity of adobe buildings made them difficult to describe in terms that conveyed their charm and appeal, yet many New Mexican authors attempted to communicate their feelings about the qualities of these structures. Taos poet Peggy Pond Church expressed sentiments shared by many writers when she wrote "Old House" in praise of adobe's ability to link men and nature. The house, like its builders Epifanio and Jesusita, seemed an integral part of the New Mexican landscape. Describing this fact she wrote,

> Time and weather here are kind to houses.
> After a space houses become one with the hillsides,
> As calm, as everlasting, as unhurried,
> The blue doorways and windows fade slowly into sky-color;
> Even Epifanio Vigil and his wife Jesusita
> Have become wind-carved and time-wrinkled and eternal.[61]

Painters, too, appreciated the scuptural quality and indigenous character of adobe structures, and painted them in every style and medium. Among the favorite subjects for artists of the regions were the adobe missions and village churches. Carlos Vierra, perhaps as interested in historical documentation as he was in creative expression, made extensive photographic studies of deteriorating Spanish missions and then painted a series of detailed pictures which realistically depicted each in its original state.[62] In contrast to Vierra, Georgia O'Keeffe removed almost all detail from the churches she painted, stressing their elemental form and inherent rhythm of linc. "Ranchos Church, Taos, New Mexico"[63] is a masterpiece of subjective interpretation. The evidences of man's association with the structure — windows, doorways, crosses — are omitted. Instead, the mission is viewed from the rear, a massive body of tons of earth rising upward from the very earth used to create it. It is evident that the architectural material, with its innate solidarity and mass, was the subject of the painting. The function of the structure is ignored. Indeed, the swelling buttresses and undulating lines of the walls are distinctly sensuous rather than sacred.

Spanish-American Arts and Crafts

In addition to Spanish-American architecture, the newly arrived Anglo painters and writers of the region soon discovered other appealing handcrafts of the Hispano.[64] Many of the newcomers adopted the use of brightly colored woven rugs and blankets, often the product of Chimayo weavers, and added Spanish colonial carved cupboards and tables to the Eastern style furnishings of their adobe homes. Although fine examples of native Spanish-American handcrafts still existed when Anglo writers and painters first settled in Santa Fe and Taos, the newcomers soon discovered that most of these objects were products of earlier years. More recently Spanish colonial crafts had suffered with the availability of inexpensive commercial substitutes. Because of their admiration for the Spanish-American culture and their aesthetic appreciation of these finely crafted art works, several artists became actively involved in the successful movement to encourage a revival of Spanish-American arts and crafts.[65]

While Anglo artists greatly admired the Hispano's secular arts of weaving and furniture carving, the art objects which seemed to have the deepest and most universal appeal were the religious carvings that decorated the village churches and homes. Isolated in a remote portion of the empire far from the centers of Spanish colonial Catholicism, hindered further by their relative poverty, the Hispanos of northern New Mexico had developed an indigenous religious folk art. Unable to obtain or afford sufficient numbers of religious statues and paintings from Mexico, the Hispanos began to carve or paint these objects themselves. At first copied from Spanish models, these *santos* (carved statues of saints or divine persons) and *retablos* (painted panels representing individuals or religious events) came to have a distinctly New Mexican style over the years.[66] The use of indigenous materials partially decreed this characteristic. Cottonwood and pine were substituted for

In the Pueblo of Taos. Oscar E. Berninghaus. Oil, 22 x 28 inches. Collection Robert E. and Evelyn McKee Foundation, El Paso, Texas.

Earth Rhythms No. 3. Raymond Jonson. 1923. Oil, 32 x 40 inches. Jonson Gallery, University of New Mexico, Albuquerque, New Mexico.

From the Faraway Nearby. Georgia O'Keeffe. 1949. Oil, 36 x 40 1/8 inches. The Metropolitan Museum of Art, the Alfred Stieglitz Collection.

Jury for the Trial of a Sheepherder for Murder. Ernest L. Blumenschein. 1936. Oil, 46 1/4 x 30 inches. Private Collection. Photography by James O. Milmoe.

both porcelain and canvas. Vegetable dyes replaced oil paints. The local character of the art was further sharpened during the period of Mexican rule when even fewer religious articles came north, and the *Santeros* (saint makers) copied from earlier New Mexican models. Although *retablos* were usually reserved for churches, *santos* were found in every villager's home.

The reasons for the appeal of *santos* to an individual artist were, of course, personal, yet several factors were obviously influential. They appealed as primitive, personal art, and as an art indigenous to the New Mexican environment. They appealed also as vivid expressions of a deeply felt religious faith. While few of the incoming artists shared the Catholic faith with his Hispanic neighbors, many sincerely admired the Hispano's commitment to that faith. The *santos* and other religious expressions of the Hispanos, Alice Henderson argued, elicited a responsive sentiment in people immersed in a less fervently devout society. The *santos* were inspired by a type of faith that seemed alien to the modern Anglo mind, yet one which was somehow "buried down deep in some remote fiber of our own race-memory."[67] Because of their varied and broad appeal, *santos* were not only collected, but also became the subject of many fine paintings. Some paintings, such as "Church Interior"[68] by Fremont Ellis, emphasize the integral role played by the objects in the Hispano's religious life. Others, such as Marsden Hartley's "El Santo"[69] and B.J.O. Nordfeldt's "Stillife With Santo,"[70] combine them with other native art objects or native plant life to emphasize the indigenous quality of the *santos*. Thus, the qualities of the *santos* which appealed most strongly to the artists were reflected in their studies of the objects.

The Hispano's Religious Faith

While the *santos* and *retablos*, like Spanish-American churches themselves, were among the favorite subjects for painters in the area, other aspects of the culture which reflected the Hispano's religious faith interested the newcomers. Because of the region's isolation, various aspects of Spanish colonial Catholicism continued to flourish in later day New Mexico Catholicism. Among these remnants of the past was the performance of religious plays. Favorite among these were nativity plays, especially "Coloquios de los Pastores," "Los Tres Reyes," and "La Aurora del Nuevo Dia."[71] These were usually performed on Christmas Eve, often in lieu of Midnight Mass in villages that had no resident priest, and were attended by families from outlying *placitas* or other villages. In later years these Hispanic folk plays, especially the Christmas pageants, were often attended by the Anglo artists.

Similar to the continuation of the religious plays in New Mexico was the survival of the *cofradia* (confraternity), a religious society composed of laymen who banded together, adopted a patron saint, and agreed to perform certain religious exercises. Because the region had been physically isolated from New Spain and the number of priests in the province was never large enough to adequately serve all the villages, over the years these societies became an increasingly integral part of the Hispano's Catholicism. This was especially true after 1821, when the newly independent Mexican government expelled all Spanish churchmen who would not swear allegiance to the new nation.[72] Again, although the Anglo newcomers were seldom Catholic themselves, they often admired the attitude of religious devotion reflected by the brotherhoods.

The Penitentes

Among the confraternities the *Hermandad de Nuestro Padre Jesus Nazareno*, more commonly known as the Penitentes, became particularly prominent. Drawing on the early Spanish tradition of physical penance and influenced by the harsh realities of the New Mexican environment, the Penitentes placed great emphasis on devotion to Christ through the sharing of His suffering. While membership was far from universal, almost every small village in northern New Mexico had a Penitente chapter. The members met regularly in a *morada* (combined meeting house and chapel) separate from the village church. Although their religious activities were carried on throughout the year, it was during the Easter season that the Penitentes were most fervent in their practices. During this season the members endured personal physical penance, and on Good Friday reenacted the crucifiction in a processional marked by flagellation and other forms of self-inflicted pain. After 1848 Catholic officials attempted to force the tempering of the rites, but in many remote villages the Penitentes continued their processionals and other Easter observances well into the twentieth century.[73]

While the authors and painters of Santa Fe and Taos were aware of the brutal aspects of the society's rituals, their admiration for the Hispano's culture as a whole and his religious sincerity in particular made it possible for many artists to artistically explore the Penitente experience with more sympathy than was usually given to the group. In her accurate yet sympathetic study of the sect entitled *Brothers of Light*, Alice Corbin Henderson included descriptions of both the gruesome Easter week rites and the Brotherhood's year round charitable work. She offered, too, a sensitive plea not for an acceptance of the practices themselves, but rather for an understanding of the sincerely religious nature of these rituals. They were practiced by a unique cultural group influenced by a unique physical environment. Mrs. Henderson described the close relationship between the environment and the rituals by noting,

> In this landscape of strange and austere beauty, the processions of the *Penitentes* have a significance of form and color which enhances the undeniably

> mystic element of their ceremonies. . . . [The land has] a beauty that is touched here in this country with a sometimes terrible sense of eternity, loneliness, and futility . . . the stark parable of the Crucification is close to the country's soul.[74]

Most importantly, she emphasized throughout her work that the Penitente rituals could not be understood unless recognized as expressions of an intense and personal religious faith, a faith which had been little affected by Renaissance, Reformation, or Rationalism. The enduring faith and the forms of its expression were inseparable, and "alike remarkable."

Painters, too, attempted to communicate in their works the depth of emotion and faith associated with the Penitente rites, and to capture the strong bond between the elemental environment and the elemental faith of the penitents. For example, in "Penitente Processional"[75] William Henderson created a portrait of the reenactment of Christ's walk to Calvary. The painting affirms the profound spiritual devotion of the Penitentes without visually stressing the physical suffering involved. At the head of the procession the *Hermano Mayor* carries a large crucifix. Behind him walks the *Rezador*, chanting the ritual from a small, well-worn book. Placed at a right angle to the leaders, the body of the procession climbs up the winding trail. Following first are the cross-bearers, bent low beneath enormous wooden crosses. Behind them walk three shrouded flagellants, naked to the waist, their white trousers streaked with blood. The interrelated nature of the men, the landscape, and the ritual is subtly suggested in many ways. The faces of the processional leaders bear a strong resemblance to the face of the crucified Christ. The hunched and penitent forms of the cross-bearers and flagellants are echoed by the rounded hills in the foreground, while the upward thrust of the crosses is matched by the higher mountain peaks in the background. The form of the cross is repeated by the branches of the cactus in the foreground, and even vaguely outlined in snow on the distant mountains. On a far distant hill, symbolizing the length of the spiritual journey as well as the physical one, stands a stark black cross. The whole procession is surrounded by the barren landscape, intensifying the mood of loneliness and solemnity of the procession. The picture as a whole is a graphic expression of the depth of both the Hispano's faith and the artist's admiration for that devotion.

The Hispano's Bond with his Land and his Community

The overwhelming importance of the Catholic religion in the Hispanic culture of northern New Mexico decreed that much of what the author wrote or the artist painted would be concerned with that faith. But there were other elements of the culture which the artists and authors of Santa Fe and Taos found admirable. Two such characteristics were his deeply felt bond to his native soil and his sense of community with his neighbors. To the Hispano, his land, however unproductive or economically unrewarding, was not merely a possession. It was conceived of as an integal part of his individual identification. The Spanish-Americans practiced division of family land among all male heirs rather than primogeniture, so that for an Hispano his land represented his birthright, an inheritance which reaffirmed who he was.[76] Such a conception tied a man firmly to an individual farm and village. The Spanish cultural trait of extended family units also helped bind him to his village. Many small mountain villages actually consisted of only a few interrelated families. The sense of community among village members was further nurtured by the demanding New Mexican environment. In semiarid New Mexico even the fertile soil of the mountian valleys needed irrigation to be productive. Construction and maintenance of irrigation ditches required communal efforts, as did the arranging and regulating of grazing and water rights. Other group efforts included construction of the church, digging of reservoirs, diversion of streams, and religious celebrations. Thus family ties and communal efforts gave the Hispano both a deep sense of communal belonging and a concurrent sense of communal responsibility. His relationship to his land and his community helped him define his personal identity.

The admiration of the Taos and Santa Fe artists for the Hispano's success in being inseparably an individual and a community member, like their admiration of the Pueblo's communal orientation, was increased by the individualistic structure of twentieth century American society. While the artists certainly believed in the need for individual self-identification and freedom, they deplored the isolation of the individual and the breakdown of community and family ties which they saw in modern America. Writing of the Hispano's combination of self and group identification, Mary Austin asserted that members of the dominant Anglo-Saxon society in the United States could benefit greatly from an understanding and acceptance of this unique characteristic. Rather than seek to make the Spanish-Americans "average installment-plan, subrotarian middle class Americans," the dominant society should recognize that Hispanos "actually achieve the thing we have deemed impossible in our European-derived social complex, individualism without competition, complete socialization without standardization."[77]

The Artists' Concern for the Hispanos

While the Anglo artists and authors admired many of the values and traditions of the Spanish-Americans of northern New Mexico and often praised these characteristics in print or paint, they were not blind to the hardships which the Hispano's way of life imposed upon him. If he felt a bond with the earth and accepted the decrees of nature, he still lived in an austere and often capricious environment. If he shared with his neighbors the land's water and pastures, he still suffered when that water failed, and the loneliness of tending flocks could drive him to madness. Perhaps more importantly, the artists were aware of the pressure placed on the individual Hispano and his culture as a whole by the increasing dominance in the region of modern Anglo society. The struggle of the sensitive Hispano to find his identity in a rapidly progressing twentieth century without totally abandoning the inheritance of his historic culture was the dominant theme in several works produced in the Santa Fe-Taos center. This conflict was the central theme in both of Raymond Otis' Santa Fe based novels. The protagonist of each novel attempts to balance the opportunities and realities of modern society with the beliefs and values of his traditional Hispanic culture. The two young men, each representing a different social status and background, take entirely different paths to similar conclusions. Lorenzo, a *rico* accepted in Anglo society, discovers that he cannot really break the bonds of his heritage ". . .emerge from the lethal past and cast his fortunes with the present."[78] The attempt brings him unhappiness rather than fulfillment. Miguel, on the other hand, intends not to abandon his mountain community, but to bring progress to it through his own advanced education and modernization. When he discovers the depth of the clash between modern Anglo culture and his own, it is the dream of changing his village that is abandoned for the contentment found in submerging himself in the most basic and ancient aspects of his Hispanic culture.[79]

OTHER REASONS FOR THE DEVELOPMENT OF THE SANTA FE-TAOS CENTER

The Tri-Cultural Character of the Towns

The deep and continuing appeal of the physical environment and the native peoples of northern New Mexico was the most important reason for the establishment and growth of an active cultural center in the region, but that appeal was not the only factor which contributed to that development. One important additional element which supported the success of the center was the tri-cultural character of the two towns. Although this feature was dependent on the presence of the Pueblos and Hispanos, it was a separate element in that it was created by the interaction of these peoples and the Anglos of the region. Unlike the typical process of "Americanization" which affected the Far West, the slow commercialization and geographic isolation of northern New Mexico allowed the native cultures to maintain their traditional forms. The vitality of the native peoples combined with the relatively slow rate of Anglo immigration into the region to create there a unique society. In Santa Fe and Taos three contrasting but complementary cultures blended and yet maintained their separate identities. Within the two towns, tolerance was a pervasive reality. Indeed, not merely tolerance, but admiration for the Indian and Hispanic cultures became a keynote for the Anglo artists and authors of the region. To the members of the art and literary colonies of Taos and Santa Fe, the tri-cultural nature of the region offered personal artistic stimulation, and additionally, an example to the dominant society of the vitalizing effect of cultural interaction. Writing in praise of the unique New Mexican cultural heritage, Alice Henderson expressed the opinion of most artists of the region when she warned against a "Main Street" mentality that would "discard or wipe out the contributions of alien races and cultures in favor of a political amalgamation which may leave only a colorless conformity in its wake."[80]

Community Acceptance of the Artists

The attitude of tolerance and acceptance which was an integral part of Santa Fe and Taos society contributed to the development of a cultural center in the region in another important way. The acceptance afforded the Indian and Hispanic peoples was also given to the Anglo artists. To some extent the traditional grouping of painters and writers into "colonies" was caused not only by their own affinity for one another, but also by society's tendency to segregate the nonconformist. John Sloan, who later spent many of his summers contentedly in Santa Fe, once complained that artists in America were "like cockroaches in kitchens — not wanted, not encouraged, but nevertheless they remain."[81] In contrast, Robert Henri said of Santa Fe, "here painters are treated with that welcome and appreciation that is supposed to exist only in certain places in Europe."[82]

The acceptance they felt encouraged the painters and writers of the two towns to become true members of the community. In Taos, for example, Mabel Luhan, although always basing her decision on what she personally considered best for the town and its inhabitants, was a generous citizen. She provided Taos with a large hospital, a bandstand for gatherings in the plaza, and innumerable books for the public library. She joined with members of the artist colony and used her considerable influence in Eastern circles to petition Washington to reroute a proposed new highway which would have destroyed half of the buildings on the square as well as numerous other old adobes.[83] Artists gave paintings to the public schools, served on the Chamber of Commerce, the volunteer fire department, and occasionally ran for mayor.[84] In Santa Fe too, painters and writers manned fire trucks and served on committees. In particular Alice Corbin Henderson supported civic projects which touched on art, architecture, writing, the annual Fiesta, and — as a friend once noted — even "a water trough for thirsty horses hitched near the plaza."[85] Numerous painters and authors joined an organization of Santa Fe and Taos citizens which worked to defeat the Bursum bill of 1921, when that piece of legislation threatened to severely reduce Pueblo land holdings and water rights.[86] In

Santa Fe and Taos the artist functioned as an active citizen as well as a creative individual.

The Western Qualities of the Region

Another influential quality of the region was the distinctly "western" atmosphere of Santa Fe and Taos. Both towns were marked by a casual style and relaxed pace of daily living. The western life style of the towns was important for several reasons. For some artists it provided an additional artistic influence through association with and interest in the animals, "cowboys," and ranching activities associated with the West. Writers, too, found stimulation in their contact with the cowboy ballad, a literary form which some authors insisted should be recognized as the "true folk poetry of the West."[87] Perhaps even more importantly, the less hectic pace of living provided the artist with the time needed for the reflection and reevaluation which produce creative works in their best forms. Writing in 1927 to explain Santa Fe's reluctance to become the summer home of a regional Chautauqua group, Mary Austin contended that residents of Santa Fe knew the difference between the type of cultural center that nurtured "definite achievement on a cultural plane," and the type that "created culture" by providing a place "to hear about what has been produced."[88] More simply, but perhaps more profoundly, Gustave Baumann asserted that "art and literature flourish wherever people give themselves time to think."[89] In Santa Fe and Taos the artist had time to think.

One other common western quality of the two towns helped to encourage the development of the cultural center. The high, dry atmosphere of the Taos-Santa Fe region provided a particularly healthful climate. It was that feature of the environment that originally brought to the towns many artists who became permanent residents. The artists Carlos Vierra and Gerald Cassidy both left New York and came to New Mexico for reasons of health, just as the poet Haniel

Long moved from Pittsburgh to Santa Fe to regain his health.[90] Alice Corbin Henderson came to Santa Fe planning to stay only until she sufficiently recovered from tuberculosis to return to her Chicago home. She in turn convinced the well known poet Witter Bynner to come to Santa Fe to recuperate from influenza. For Bynner, as for Alice Henderson, the residence became permanent.[91]

The Attitudes and Motivations of the Artists

The appeal of elements indigenous to the region, especially the physical environment and native peoples, certainly played an indispensable role in the development of the Santa Fe-Taos cultural center. The attractive character of these elements, however, was intensified by factors independent of the New Mexican setting. Perhaps most important among these external influences were the attitudes and motivations of the writers and painters themselves. Many of these individuals shared the general discontentment with industrialized American society and its art forms which was widespread among creative intellectuals during the period.[92] The early decades of the twentieth century was a period of dramatic social change. Within the dominant society of the United States increasing industrialization and urbanization was rapidly destroying both the traditional rural community and the sense of belonging which community membership had once given the individual. The dehumanization which seemed to be an integral part of the machine age, and which was furthered by the disillusionment that followed the first World War, was isolating the individual. American society as a whole seemed to have lost any sense of unity or community. National devotion to individualism, often in its most self-serving form, had resulted in separation and alienation of society's members. To many artists the New Mexican environment offered an indigenous and elemental contrast to the rootless and artificial climate of urbanized America. The sense of identity and belonging the Hispano and Pueblo gained from devotion to his religion, community, and land sharply exposed the feelings of disunity, alienation and isolation experienced by many individuals within American society. Faced with these contrasts, the artists and authors of Santa Fe and Taos called on the members of the dominant culture to learn from the achievements of the New Mexican peoples and return to a sincere communion with their native land and their fellow man.

Favorable reaction to northern New Mexico was even further strengthened for some artists because of their discontentment with American art of the period. Many of the incoming artists desired to develop an art freed from European models and influence. The native cultures and magnificent physical environment provided these artists with inspirational contact with truly indigenous American elements. Indian and Hispanic art forms — dance, music, pottery, painting, carving — were all native forms of American art. While the artists did not wish to copy this art, they did seek their personal inspiration from the same elements which inspired Indian and Hispanic art. For many artists the desire for this contact with indigenous arts and sources of inspiration was a vital factor in tying them firmly to the region.

The motivations and attitudes of the incoming writers and painters had an important influence on the development of the center in one other way. Because these artists found so much to admire in the region, they soon became propagandists for the two towns, and through their activities and invitations drew additional creative people to the center. Particularly active in this way were Alice Corbin Henderson of Santa Fe and Mabel Dodge Luhan of Taos. Through the friendships she had made while an editor of *Poetry* in Chicago, Alice Henderson encouraged dozens of well known writers to visit Santa Fe frequently or to stay for extended periods. Similarly, Mabel Luhan brought to Taos such creative individuals as Andrew Dasburg, Georgia O'Keeffe, Leopold

Stokowski, Leo Stein, John Marin, and D. H. Lawrence. Through such activities the size and the reputation of the center was increased.

CONCLUSIONS

Between 1898 and the beginning of the second World War, painters, poets, playwrights, and novelists arrived in Santa Fe and Taos from every section of the United States. During these years, active colonies of writers and painters flourished in both towns. The factors which contributed to the establishment and continued growth of these colonies were numerous, but to a great degree they were all closely interrelated. Most basic to the development of the center was the beauty and power of the physical environment and the presence in the region of the Spanish-American and Pueblo Indian peoples. Each of these elements — the Indian, the Hispano, and the environment — offered tremendous visual stimulation to artists, but each also appealed on a deeper level. The elemental character of the land and the indigenous nature, enduring religious faith, and communal-centered orientation of the Indian and Hispanic peoples were admired for their own intrinsic value beyond their artistic appeal.

Several elements that were independent of the northern New Mexican region served to intensify the appeal of the area to the incoming artists. Of particular importance was the general dissatisfaction among creative intellectuals of the period with many elements of American society. To artists and authors who were members of a society struggling with the forces of industrialization, war, and dehumanization, the elemental land and its enduring cultures seemed to offer alternative approaches to many basic problems of the period. Similarly, the increasing desire among artists to create a distinctly American art derived from an American aesthetic tradition increased the favorable reaction to the indigenous environment, cultures, and art forms of the region.

In addition all these elements, the development of the cultural center was further nurtured by several other factors. Santa Fe and Taos provided a stimulating tri-cultural setting, a reflective atmosphere, and personal acceptance of the artists and authors. Further, the members of the literary and artist colonies in each town themselves contributed to their growth through their own actions. Through exhibition of their works or by personal invitation the resident artists drew additional creative people to the area. Thus the uniquely attracting elements of the region, the intellectual climate of the period, and the personal motivations of the incoming artists blended together to nurture the creation of a vital and productive American cultural center in Santa Fe and Taos, New Mexico, during the early decades of the twentieth century.

Taos Society of Artists, 1927. Standing, left to right: Martin Hennings, Bert Phillips, Victor Higgins, Ernest Blumenschein, Joseph H. Sharp. Seated, left to right: Walter Ufer, Irving Couse, Oscar Berninghaus, Herbert Dunton, Kenneth Adams. Photo courtesy The Thomas Gilcrease Institute of American History and Art, Tulsa, Oklahoma.

Cliff Dwellings No. 3. Raymond Jonson. 1927. Oil, 48 x 38 inches. Jonson Gallery, University of New Mexico, Albuquerque, New Mexico.

NOTES

1 Josiah Gregg, *Commerce of the Prairies: A Selection*, ed. David Freeman Hawke (New York: Bobbs-Merrill Co., Inc., 1970), p. 64.

2 Numerous articles concerning the Taos art colony or individual Taos or Santa Fe painters can be found in such journals as *International Studio, American Artist, The American Magazine of Art, Survey Graphic, Western Historical Quarterly*, and *The American West*. Biographies of several of the painters also exist. For more general studies of the artists of the region see Laura M. Bickerstaff, *Pioneer Artists of Taos* (Denver: Sage Books, 1955); Van Deren Coke, *Taos and Santa Fe: The Artist's Environment, 1882-1942* (Albuquerque: University of New Mexico Press, 1963); and, Edna Robertson and Sara Nestor, *Artists of Canyons and Caminos: Santa Fe, The Early Years* (Layton, Utah: Peregrine Smith, Inc., 1976); Mary Carroll Nelson, *The Legendary Artists of Taos* (New York: Watson-Guptill, 1980; and Patricia Janis Broder, *Taos: A Painter's Dream* (Boston: New York Graphic Society, 1980). No full length study of the literary colonies in the two towns has as yet been published, but numerous biographies or autobiographies of the individual writers are available. Similarly, to date there is no published study of the cultural center as a whole, dealing with the authors as well as painters and their common motivations. For such a study see Kay Aiken Reeve "The Making of an American Place: The Development of Santa Fe and Taos, New Mexico as An American Cultural Center, 1898-1942," Diss. Texas A&M 1977. Unless otherwise cited, general statements in this paper concerning the writers of the region are drawn from this source.

3 Because the general facts concerning the artist colonies in the two towns have been so widely published (see Bickerstaff; Coke; Robertson and Nestor) only lesser-known points are specifically referenced in this general description of the establishment of the cultural center.

4 The production of "traditional western paintings" was encouraged by the good market for such paintings. For an excellent study of the support the more traditional artists of the region received, especially financial support, see Keith L. Bryant, "The Atchison, Topeka, and Santa Fe Railway and the Development of the Taos and Santa Fe Art Colonies," *Western Historical Quarterly*, 9, No. 4 (October 1978), pp. 437-453.

5 Lincoln Steffens, *The Autobiography of Lincoln Steffens* (New York: Harcourt, Brace, 1931), p. 655.

6 Witter Bynner and Oliver La Farge, eds., "Alice Henderson: An Appreciation," *New Mexico Quarterly*, 19 (Spring 1949), pp. 35-79.

7 The terms Pueblo, Spanish-American, Hispano, and Anglo are used in this study in the manner they have been used in northern New Mexico for centuries. Pueblo refers to an individual Indian or to the Indian group as a whole. The term pueblo, in lower case, refers to the traditional communal dwellings (village) of these Indians. While wide variations in preference exist among individuals in the ethnic group, both the terms Hispano and Spanish-American are widely used with reference to the Spanish speaking (non-Indian) people of the region. Those terms are used interchangeably in this study. Similarly, the general term Anglo has long been used to identify non-Spanish, non-Indian individuals in the region, whether they were American, European, black or white. It is used in that manner in this study.

8 Marsden Hartley, "Aesthetic Sincerity," *El Palacio*, 5 (December 9, 1918), p. 33.

9 As quoted in Sheldon Reich, "John Marin and the Piercing Light of Taos," *Art News*, 73 (January 1974), p. 16.

10 Mary Austin, "Why I Live in Santa Fe," *The Golden Book Magazine* 16 (October 1932), p. 306.

11 Mabel Dodge Luhan, *Intimate Memories, IV, Edge of Taos Desert: An Escape to Reality* (New York: Harcourt, Brace, 1937), pp. 32-33.

12 David Herbert Lawrence, *Phoenix: The Posthumous Papers of D.H. Lawrence*, Edward D. McDonald, ed. (New York: Viking Press, 1936), p. 142.

13 Although all Pueblo groups share many common cultural traits there are numerous differences among the various pueblos. Of particular importance is the basic division of the Pueblos into Eastern (Rio Grande Valley) and Western groupings. While the differences are important, they are more easily recognized by an anthropologist than an artist. The description of Pueblo cutlure in this study is based upon the most basic and most often shared elements of the culture as it was functioning in the early 1900s. This generalization is primarily drawn from the following important sources: Adolph E. Bandelier and Edgar L. Hewett, *Indians of the Rio Grande Valley* (Albuquerque: University of New Mexico Press, 1937); Elsie Clews Parsons, *Pueblo Indian Religion* 2 vols. (Chicago: University of Chicago Press, 1939); Edward P. Dozier, *The Pueblo Indians of North America*, Case Studies in Cultural Anthropology (New York: Holt, Rinehart and Winston, 1970).

14 Bickerstaff, p. 23.

15 Author's Interview with Barbara Latham, January 12, 1976, Roswell, New Mexico.

16 Author's Interview with Fremont Ellis, January 7 and 11, 1976, Santa Fe, New Mexico.

17 Sheldon Parsons as quoted in Pat Trenton, *Picturesque Images from Taos and Santa Fe* (Denver: The Denver Art Museum, 1974).

18 Ellis Interview.

19 For a broad treatment exploring the disenchantment of intellectuals of the period see Christopher Lasch, *The New Radicalism in America (1889-1963): The Intellectual as a Social Type* (New York: Knopf, 1963).

20 Jonathan Scott, "Interview with Andrew Dasburg," *Black Bear Review*, 1 (Winter 1975), p. 2.

21 Charlotte Trego, "Andrew Dasburg — At One with His Environment," *New Mexico Magazine*, 53 (August 1975), p. 25.

22 Author's Interview with Emil Bisttram, December 20, 1975, Taos, New Mexico.

23 Alfred Morang, *Transcendental Painting* (Santa Fe: privately printed 1940), n.p.

24 Author's Interview with Raymond Jonson, January 6, 1976, Albuquerque, New Mexico. For an excellent study of Mr. Jonson's development as an artist see Ed Garman, *Raymond Jonson: Painter* (Albuquerque: University of New Mexico Press, 1976).

25 Mabel Dodge Luhan, *Winter in Taos* (New York: Harcourt, Brace, 1935).

26 Luhan, *Taos Desert*, p. 10.

27 As quoted in Coke, p. 52; John Marin, *Letters of John Marin*, ed. Herbert J. Seligman (1931; rpt. New York: Greenwood Press, 1970), n.p., Marin to Stieglitz, July 21, 1929, Taos, New Mexico.

28 Informative discussions of Miss O'Keeffe's work can be found in her own *Georgia O'Keeffe* (New York: Viking Press, 1976), and the recent biography by Laurie Lisle, *Portrait of an Artist: Georgia O'Keeffe* (New York: Pocket Books, 1981).

29 Alice Corbin [Henderson], *Red Earth* (Chicago: Ralph Fletcher Seymour, 1920), pp. 15-16. Throughout her career as an editor, essayist, and poet, Alice Corbin Henderson wrote poetry under the name of Alice Corbin, and prose in the name of Alice Corbin Henderson, usually abbreviated A. C. H.

30 Henderson, *Red Earth*, p. 13.

31 Mabel Dodge Luhan, "Paso por Aqui," *New Mexico Quarterly*, 21 (Summer 1951), 137-146; Mabel Dodge Luhan, *Taos and Its Artists* (New York: Duell, Sloan, and Pearce, 1947).

32 Bisttram Interview.

33 Luhan, *Winter*, p. 78; Luhan, *Taos Desert*, p. 231.

34 The ability of the Pueblo Indians to maintain the integrity of their religion far into the twentieth century is due in part to their protection of it from too deep a scrutiny by outsiders. For that reason Edward Dozier's *The Pueblo Indians of North America* is a particularly valuable source, as the author is himself a Pueblo Indian. For his comments on Pueblo religion see Dozier, pp. 182-187; 200-217. The general description of the Pueblo religion in this study is drawn from Dozier's work and from Parsons, *Pueblo Indian Religion* and Bandelier and Hewett, pp. 15-20.

35 Jonson Interview.

36 University of New Mexico Collection.

37 Lawrence, p. 146.

38 Lawrence, p. 147.

39 Luhan, *Taos Desert*, p. 101.

40 Luhan, *Winter*, p. 196.

41 Collection of Eugene D. Adkins.

42 Alice Corbin Henderson, "Dance Rituals of the Pueblo Indians," *Theater Arts Magazine*, 7 (April 1923), pp. 109, 110.

43 Henderson, "Rituals," p. 114.

44 For an informative discussion of Pueblo architecture and its relation to nature see Vincent Scully, *Pueblo: Mountain, Village, and Dance* (New York: Viking Press, 1975).

45 Mary Austin, "Cults of the Pueblos: An Interpretation of Some Native Ceremonials," *Century Magazine*, 109 (November 1924), p. 35.

46 Sherwood Anderson, *Mid-American Chants* (New York: John Lane Company, 1918).

47 Mary Austin to Alice Corbin Henderson, January 8, no yr., in The Alice Corbin Henderson Papers, now located (since 1978) in Humanities Research Center, The University of Texas at Austin. The author wishes to express her appreciation to Mrs. Alice Rossin for permission to examine the collection when it was located at El Cuervo Ranch, Tesuque, New Mexico.

48 Luhan, *Taos Desert*, pp. 63-64.

49 The revival of both pottery making and painting among the Pueblos was greatly encouraged by anthropologists and artists alike. For a discussion of the role played by Dr. Edgar L. Hewett and the School of American Research in encouraging this revitalization see Bandelier and Hewett, pp. 63-67.

50 Van Wyck Brooks, *John Sloan: A Painter's Life* (New York: E. P. Dutton, 1955), pp. 159-160, 167.

51 *Exposition of Indian Tribal Arts at Grand Central Art Galleries* (New York, n.p., 1931), pamphlet in Henderson Papers.

52 Ralph M. Pearson, *The Modern Renaissance in American Art* (New York: Harper, 1954), p. 42; Coke, p. 31.

53 Jonson Interview.

54 Brooks, p. 167; Marsden Hartley, "The Scientific Esthetic of the Red Man," *Art and Archeology*, 13 (March 1922), p. 119.

55 Richard McLanathan, *Art in America: A Brief History* (New York: Harcourt, Brace, Jovanavich, Inc., 1973), pp. 188-189.

56 Randolph Bourne as quoted in Robert E. Spiller, *A Time of Harvest: American Literature, 1910-1960* (New York: Hill and Wang, 1962), p. 2.

57 For an excellent study of literary "Regionalism" in the early twentieth century see Cary McWilliams, *The New Regionalism In American Literature* (Seattle: University of Washington Bookstore, 1930); Also see B. A. Botkin, "Regionalism: Cult or Culture?" *The English Journal*, 25 (March 1936), pp. 181-185.

58 Sociologists disagree as to how distinct the Spanish-American or Hispanic culture of northern New Mexico is in relation to the culture of Mexico or other Latin American countries. For a discussion of this debate see Nancy L. Gonzales, *The Spanish-Americans of New Mexico: A Heritage of Pride* (Albuquerque: University of New Mexico Press, 1969), pp. 197-213. Also see Erna Fergusson, *New Mexico: A Pageant of Three Peoples* (Albuquerque: University of New Mexico Press, 1976); Marta Weigle, ed., *Hispanic Villages of Northern New Mexico: A Reprint of Volume II of the 1933 Tewa Basin Study* (Santa Fe: Lightning Tree Press, 1975); and, Roland Dickey, *New Mexico Village Arts* (Albuquerque: University of New Mexico Press, 1949). The generalized description of the Spanish-American culture in northern New Mexico in this study is drawn from the above cited references.

59 For a concise treatment of New Mexican architecture as it developed through the centuries see Federal Writers' Project, *New Mexico: a Guide to a Colorful State* (Albuquerque: University of New Mexico Press, 1945), pp. 148-155. Also see Bainbridge Bunting, *Taos Adobes* (Santa Fe: Museum of New Mexico Press, 1964), *Early Architecture in New Mexico* (Albuquerque: University of New Mexico Press, 1976); *Of Earth and Timbers Made* (Albuquerque: University of New Mexico Press, 1974); and Dickey, pp. 33-50.

60 Ellis Interview.

61 In Benjamin A. Botkin, ed., *Southwest Scene: An Anthology of Regional Verse* (Oklahoma City: The Economy Co., 1931), p. 22.

62 Coke, p. 27.

63 Amon Carter Museum of Western Art.

64 The most informative overview of Spanish-American arts remains Dickey's *New Mexico Village Arts*.

65 The Spanish-American arts of woodcarving, weaving, and tin work all experienced a distinct revival in the 1920s. As they had done in the revival of Pueblo arts, the Anglo artists of Santa Fe and Taos played an important supportive role in this renewal of native arts. For information concerning that role, see Withers Woolford, "Revival of the Native Crafts," *New Mexico Magazine*, 9 (September 1931), pp. 24-26; Frank Applegate, "Spanish Colonial Arts," *Survey*, 66 (May 1, 1931), pp. 156-157; and Alice Corbin Henderson, "Furniture for Colonial Spanish Homes," *House and Garden*, 59 (July 1928), pp. 62, 92, 106.

66 For excellent studies of these objects see Dickey, pp. 137-166; and, Elizabeth Boyd, *Saints and Saintmakers* (Santa Fe: Laboratory of Anthropology, 1946).

67 Alice Corbin Henderson, *Brothers of Light: The Penitentes of the Southwest* (1937; rpt. Santa Fe: William Gannon, 1977), p. 14.

68 Collection of Eugene B. Adkins.

69 Museum of New Mexico.

70 Collection of Eleanor and Van Deren Coke.

71 Aurora Lucero-White Lea, *Literary Folklore of the Hispanic Southwest* (San Antonio: Naylor, 1953). Although scholars have traced the origins of specific New Mexican folk plays to sixteenth or seventeenth century Mexico rather than to Spain, the tradition doubtlessly dates back to the Morality and Miracle Plays of Medieval Europe.

72 Dozier, pp. 93-94.

73 For detailed scholarly coverage of the sect see Carlos E. Cortez, ed., *The Penitentes of New Mexico* (New York: Arno Press, 1974); Marta Weigle, *Brothers of Light, Brothers of Blood* (Albuquerque: University of New Mexico Press, 1976); and Marta Weigle, *A Penitente Bibliography* (Albuquerque: University of New Mexico Press, 1976).

74 Henderson, *Brothers*, pp. 13, 49.

75 Museum of New Mexico.

76 Tomas C. Atencion, "The Human Dimensions in Land Use and Displacement in Northern New Mexican Villages," in Clark S. Knowlton, ed., *Indian and Spanish-American Adjustments to Arid and Semiarid Environments* (Lubbock: Texas Technological College, 1964), p. 45.

77 Mary Austin, "Mexicans and New Mexico," *Survey*, 66 (May 1, 1931), p. 190.

78 Raymond Otis, *Fire in the Night* (New York: Farrar and Rinehart, 1934), p. 19.

79 Raymond Otis, *Miguel of the Bright Mountain* (Albuquerque: University of New Mexico Press, 1977)p. 315. (Zia Series Reprint)

80 Alice Corbin Henderson, "The New Mexico Tradition in Southwest Literature," unpublished TS in Henderson Papers.

81 Brooks, p. 198.

82 As quoted in "New Mexico Fine Arts," *The Santa Fean*, 2 (September 1974), p. 27.

83 Claire Morrill, *A Taos Mosaic: Portrait of a New Mexico Village* (Albuquerque: University of New Mexico Press, 1973), pp. 110, 113.

84 Bisttram Interview; Author's Interview with Howard Cook, January 12, 1976, Roswell, New Mexico.

85 Ruth Laughlin, "Santa Fe in the Twenties," in Bynner and La Farge, "Appreciation," p. 59.

86 For a brief explanation of the Bursum Bill and the involvement of the members of the art and literary colonies in its defeat see Oliver La Farge, *Santa Fe: The Autobiography of a Southwestern Town* (Norman: University of Oklahoma Press, 1959), pp. 274-281.

87 Alice Corbin Henderson, "The Folk Poetry of These States," *Poetry*, 14, No. 5 (August 1920), pp. 264-273.

88 Mary Austin, "The Town That Doesn't Want a Chautauqua," *The New Republic*, 47 (July 7, 1926), p. 196.

89 Gustave Baumann and Calla Hay, *Gustave Baumann* (Santa Fe: Museum of New Mexico, 1972), p. 28.

90 Coke, p. 27; Trenton, p. 45; "Haniel Long" in Stanly J. Kunitz, ed., *Twentieth Century Authors: A Biographical Dictionary of Modern Literature* (New York: Wilson, 1942), p. 846.

91 Witter Bynner, "Alice and I," in Bynner and La Farge, "Appreciation," pp. 36 37.

92 For informative discussions of the major readjustments of philosophy among intellectuals, writers, and artists of the period see the previously cited works by Lasch, Spiller and McLanathan.

BIBLIOGRAPHY

PRIMARY SOURCES

MANUSCRIPT COLLECTIONS

The Alice Corbin Henderson Papers. Humanities Research Center, The University of Texas, Austin, Texas.

The Willard "Spud" Johnson Papers. Humanities Research Center, The University of Texas, Austin, Texas.

The Mabel Dodge Luhan Papers. Humanities Research Center, The University of Texas, Austin, Texas.

INTERVIEWS

Bisttram, Emil; December 20, 1975, Taos, New Mexico.

Blumenschein, Helen; December 20, 1975, Taos, New Mexico.

Cook, Howard, and Barbara Latham; January 12, 1976, Roswell, New Mexico.

Ellis, Fremont; January 7 and 11, 1976, Santa Fe, New Mexico.

Jonson, Raymond; January 6, 1976, Albuquerque, New Mexico.

BOOKS AND PAMPHLETS

Austin, Mary. *Land of Journey's Ending.* New York: Century, 1924.

Baumann, Gustave and Calla Hay. *Gustave Baumann.* Santa Fe: Museum of New Mexico, 1972.

Brett, Dorothy. *Lawrence and Brett: A Friendship.* Philadelphia: Lippincott, 1933.

Bynner, Witter. *Indian Earth.* New York: Knopf, 1929.

Henderson, Alice Corbin. *A Boy Painter Among the Pueblo Indians.* New York: Eastern Association of Indian Affairs, [1926].

―――. *Brothers of Light. The Penitentes of the Southwest.* New York: Harcourt, Brace, 1937.

―――. *Red Earth.* Chicago: Ralph Fletcher Seymour, 1920.

―――. *The Sun Turns West.* Santa Fe: Writers' Editions, 1933.

―――, ed. *The Turquoise Trail: An Anthology of New Mexico Poetry.* Boston and New York: Houghton Mifflin, 1928.

The Indian Arts Fund: Santa Fe: Indian Arts Fund, n.d.

Johnson, Willard [Spud]. *Horizontal Yellow*. Santa Fe: Writers' Editions, 1935.

Lawrence, David Herbert. *Phoenix: The Posthumous Papers of D. H. Lawrence*. Edited by Edward C. McDonald. New York: Viking Press, 1968.

Lawrence, Frieda. *Memoirs and Correspondence*. Edited by E. W. Tedlock, Jr. New York: Knopf, 1964.

———. *Not I But The Wind*. London: Heinemann, 1934.

Long, Haniel. *Atlantides*. Santa Fe: Writers' Editions, 1933.

———. *Interlinear to Cabeza de Vaca*. Santa Fe: Writers' Editions, 1936.

Luhan, Mabel Dodge. *Intimate Memories*. Vol. 1. *Background*. New York: Harcourt, Brace, 1933.

———. *Intimate Memories*. Vol. 2. *European Experiences*. New York: Harcourt, Brace, 1935.

———. *Intimate Memories*. Vol. 3. *Movers and Shakers*. New York: Harcourt, Brace, 1936.

———. *Intimate Memories*. Vol. 4. *On the Edge of Taos Desert: An Escape to Reality*. New York: Harcourt, Brace, 1937.

———. *Lorenzo in Taos*. New York: Knopf, 1932.

———. *Taos and Its Artists*. New York: Duell, Sloan and Pearce, 1947.

———. *Winter in Taos*. New York: Harcourt, Brace, 1935.

Marin, John. *Letters of John Marin*. Edited by Herbert J. Seligman. New York: Privately Printed, 1931 (Reprinted by Greenwood Reprinting, 1970).

Otis, Raymond. *Fire in the Night*. New York: Farrar and Rinehart, 1934.

———. *Miguel of the Bright Mountain*. Albuquerque: University of New Mexico Press, 1977.

Steffens, Lincoln. *The Autobiography of Lincoln Steffens*. New York: Harcourt, Brace, 1931.

PERIODICAL ARTICLES

Adams, Kenneth. "Los Ocho Pintores." *New Mexico Quarterly* 21 (Summer 1951), pp. 146-152.

Applegate, Frank D. "Spanish Colonial Arts." *Survey* 66 (May 1, 1931), pp. 156-157.

Austin, Mary. "Cults of the Pueblos: An Interpretation of Some Native Ceremonials." *Century Magazine* 109 (November 1924), pp. 28-35.

―――――. "Mexicans and New Mexico." *Survey* 66 (May 1, 1931), pp. 141-144, 187-190.

―――――. "The Town that Doesn't Want a Chautauqua." *The New Republic* 47 (July 7, 1926), pp. 195-197.

―――――. "Why I Live in Santa Fe." *The Golden Book Magazine* 16 (October 1932), pp. 306-307.

Brett, Dorothy. "Painting Indians." *New Mexico Quarterly* 21 (Summer 1951), pp. 167-173.

Bynner, Witter, and Oliver La Farge, eds. "Alice Henderson: An Appreciation." *New Mexico Quarterly* 19 (Spring 1949), pp. 35-79.

Hartley, Marsden. "Aesthetic Sincerity." *El Palacio* 5 (December 9, 1918), pp. 332-333.

―――――. "America as Landscape." *El Palacio* 5 (December 21, 1918), pp. 340-343.

―――――. "The Scientific Esthetic of the Red Man." *Art and Archeology* 13 (March 1922), pp. 113-119.

Henderson, Alice Corbin. "Dance Rituals of the Pueblo Indians." *Theatre Arts Magazine* 7 (April 1923), pp. 109-114.

―――――. "The Folk Poetry of These States." *Poetry* 14, No. 5. (August 1920, pp. 264-273.

―――――. "Furniture for Colonial Spanish Homes." *House and Garden* 59 (July 1928), pp. 62, 92, 106.

Luhan, Mabel Dodge. "Paso Por Aqui." *New Mexico Quarterly* 21 (Summer 1951), pp. 137-146.

SECONDARY MATERIALS

UNPUBLISHED THESES AND DISSERTATIONS

Black, Dorothy S. "A Study of Taos as an Art Colony and of Representative Taos Painters." Master's thesis, University of New Mexico, 1959.

Reeve, Kay Aiken. "The Making of an American Place: The Development of Santa Fe and Taos, New Mexico, as an American Cultural Center, 1898-1942." Ph.D. dissertation, Texas A&M University, 1977.

Stevens, Walter S. "John Marin: The New Mexico Period." Master's thesis, University of New Mexico, 1967.

BOOKS AND PAMPHLETS

Anderson, Sherwood. *Mid-American Chants*. New York: John Lane Company, 1918.

Bandelier, Adolph F. and Edgar L. Hewett. *Indians of the Rio Grande Valley*. New York: Cooper Square Publishers, 1973.

Bickerstaff, Laura M. *Pioneer Artists of Taos*. Denver: Sage Books, 1955.

Botkin, Benjamin A., ed. *Southwest Scene: An Anthology of Regional Verse*. Oklahoma City: The Economy Co., 1931.

Boyd, Elizabeth. *Saints and Saintmakers of New Mexico*. Santa Fe: Laboratory of Anthropology, 1946.

Broder, Patricia J. *Taos: A Painter's Dream*. Boston: New York Graphic Society, 1980.

Brooks, Van Wyck. *John Sloan: A Painter's Life*. New York: E. P. Dutton, 1955.

Bunting, Bainbridge. *Early Architecture in New Mexico*. Albuquerque: University of New Mexico Press, 1976.

_____. *Of Earth and Timber Made: New Mexico Architecture*. Albuquerque: University of New Mexico Press, 1974.

_____. *Taos Adobes*. Santa Fe: Museum of New Mexico Press, 1964.

Calvin, Ross. *Sky Determines*. Albuquerque: University of New Mexico Press, 1948.

Coke, Van Deren. *Andrew Dasburg*. Albuquerque: University of New Mexico Press, 1979.

_____. *Taos and Santa Fe: The Artist's Environment, 1882-1942*. Albuquerque: University of New Mexico Press, 1963.

Cortez, Carlos E., ed. *The Penitentes of New Mexico*. New York: Arno Press, 1974.

Dickey, Roland. *New Mexico Village Arts*. Albuquerque: University of New Mexico Press, 1949.

Dozier, Edward P. *The Pueblo Indians of North America*. New York: Holt, Rinehart, and Winston, 1970.

Eggan, Frederick. *Social Organization of the Western Pueblos*. Chicago: University of Chicago Press, 1931.

Federal Writers' Project. *New Mexico: A Guide to a Colorful State*. Albuquerque: University of New Mexico Press, 1945.

Fergusson, Erna. *New Mexico: A Pageant of Three Peoples*. New York: Knopf, 1951.

Garman, Ed. *The Art of Raymond Jonson: Painter*. Albuquerque: University of New Mexico Press, 1976.

Gonzalez, Nancie L. *The Spanish-Americans of New Mexico: A Heritage of Pride*. Albuquerque: University of New Mexico Press, 1969.

Gregg, Josiah. *Commerce of the Prairies*. Edited by Max Moorhead. Norman: University of Oklahoma Press, 1954.

Hewett, Edgar L. and Bertha P. Dutton. *The Pueblo Indian World*. Albuquerque: University of New Mexico Press, 1948.

Jones, Billy Mac. *Health Seekers in the Southwest, 1817-1900*. Norman: University of Oklahoma Press, 1967.

Knowlton, Clark S., ed. *Indian and Spanish-American Adjustments to Arid and Semiarid Environments*. Lubbock: Texas Technological College, 1964.

Kunitz, Stanley J., ed. *Twentieth Century Authors, a Biographical Dictionary of Modern Literature*. New York: Wilson, 1942.

LaFarge, Oliver. *Santa Fe: Autobiography of a Southwestern Town*. Norman: University of Oklahoma Press, 1959.

Lasch, Christopher. *The New Radicalism in America: 1889-1963: The Intellectual as a Social Type*. New York: Knopf, 1965.

Lea, Aurora Lucero-White. *Literary Folklore of the Hispanic Southwest*. San Antonio: Naylor, 1953.

Lisle, Laurie. *Portrait of an Artist: Georgia O'Keeffe*. New York: Pocket Books, 1981.

Lyday, Jo W. *Mary Austin: The Southwest Works*. Austin: Steck-Vaughn, 1968.

McLanathan, Richard. *Art in America: A Brief History*. New York: Harcourt, Brace, Jovanovich, Inc., 1973.

McWilliams, Cary. *The New Regionalism in American Literature*. Seattle: University of Washington Bookstore, 1930.

Morrill, Claire. *A Taos Mosaic: Portrait of a New Mexico Village*. Albuquerque: University of New Mexico Press, 1973.

Morang, Alfred. *Transcendental Painting*. Santa Fe: N.P., 1940.

Nelson, Mary Carroll. *The Legendary Artists of Taos*. New York: Watson-Guptill, 1980.

O'Keeffe, Georgia. *Georgia O'Keeffe*. New York: Viking Press, 1976.

Parsons, Elsie Clews. *Pueblo Indian Religion*. 2 Vols. Chicago: University of Chicago Press, 1939.

Pearce, Thomas M. *Alice Corbin Henderson.* Austin: Steck-Vaughn, 1969.

Pearson, Ralph M. *The Modern Renaissance in American Art.* New York: Harper, 1954.

Robertson, Edna C. *Los Cinco Pintores.* Santa Fe: Museum of New Mexico, 1975.

_____ and Sarah Nestor. *Artists of Canyons and Caminos: Santa Fe, The Early Years.* Layton, Utah: Peregrine Smith, Inc., 1976.

Sanchez, George I. *Forgotten People: A Study of New Mexicans.* Albuquerque: University of New Mexico Press, 1940.

Scully, Vincent. *Pueblo: Mountain, Village, and Dance.* New York: Viking Press, 1975.

Spiller, Robert. *A Time of Harvest: American Literature, 1910-1960.* New York: Hill and Wang, 1962.

Weigle, Marta. *A Penitente Bibliography.* Albuquerque: University of New Mexico Press, 1976.

_____, *Brothers of Light, Brothers of Blood: The Penitentes of the Southwest.* Albuquerque: University of New Mexico Press, 1976.

_____, ed. *Hispanic Villages of Northern New Mexico: A Reprint of Volume II of the 1935 Tewa Basin Study.* Santa Fe: Lightning Tree, 1975.

CATALOGS OF EXHIBITIONS

Branham, Eva Fechin. *Nicolai Fechin.* Santa Fe: N.P., 1975.

Ewing, Robert E. *Victor Higgins: 1884-1949.* Santa Fe: Museum of New Mexico, 1972.

Exposition of Indian Tribal Arts at Grand Central Art Galleries. New York: Exposition of Indian Tribal Arts, Inc., 1931.

Rossin, Alice [Henderson]. *William Penhallow Henderson: 1877-1943, Retrospective Exhibition.* Santa Fe: Museum of New Mexico, 1963.

Trenton, Pat. *Picturesque Images from Taos and Santa Fe.* Denver: Denver Art Museum, 1974.

PERIODICAL ARTICLES

Botkin, B.A. "Regionalism: Cult or Culture?" *The English Journal* 25 (March 1936), pp. 181-185.

Bryant, Keith. "The Atchison, Topeka, and Santa Fe Railway and The Development of the Taos and Santa Fe Art Colonies." *Western Historical Quarterly* 9, No. 4 (October 1978), pp. 437-453.

Cassidy, Ina Sizer. "Art and Artists of New Mexico: Handcrafts Center." *New Mexico Magazine* 19 (May 1941), pp. 23, 35-36.

Chavez, Fray Angelico. "The Penitentes of New Mexico." *New Mexico Historical Review* 29 (April 1954), pp. 97-123.

Metzgar, Joseph W. "The Ethnic Sensitivity of Spanish New Mexicans: A Survey and Analysis." *New Mexico Historical Review* 49 (January 1974), pp. 49-73.

"New Mexico Fine Arts Museum." *The Santa Fean* 2 (September 1974), pp. 25-27.

Reich, Sheldon. "John Marin and the Piercing Light of Taos." *Art News* 73 (January 1974), pp. 16-17.

Scott, Johnathan. "Interview with Andrew Dasburg." *The Black Bear Review* 1 (Winter 1975), pp. 1-10.

Trego, Charlotte. "Andrew Dasburg — At One with His Environment." *New Mexico Magazine* 53 (August 1975), pp. 25-27.

Woolford, Withers. "Revival of the Native Crafts." *New Mexico Magazine* 9 (September 1931), pp. 24-26.

TEXAS WESTERN PRESS

*gratefully acknowledges
the following endowments:*

THE MARY HANNER REDFORD MEMORIAL FUND
THE JUDGE AND MRS. ROBERT E. CUNNINGHAM FUND
THE DR. C. L. SONNICHSEN SOUTHWESTERN PUBLICATION FUND

*all of which make possible
this and other issues of*

SOUTHWESTERN STUDIES